Ephesians

A Journey into God's Secret Plan

Jim Bryden

O&U
Onwards & Upwards

Ephesians

Onwards and Upwards Publishers

3 Radfords Turf, Cranbrook, Exeter,
EX5 7DX, United Kingdom.
www.onwardsandupwards.org

First edition, published in the United Kingdom by Onwards and Upwards Publishers (2019).

ISBN:	978-1-78815-717-9
Typeface:	Sabon LT
Editor:	Hilja Jeffery
Graphic design:	LM Graphic Design

The views and opinions expressed in this book are the author's own, and do not necessarily represent the views and opinions of Onwards and Upwards Publishers or its staff.

Endorsements

Jim Bryden invites us to join him on an exciting *Journey of Faith* – and proves to be a well-informed and enthusiastic guide. He helps us discover new spiritual riches in Paul's Letter to the Ephesians, offering a devotional commentary that blends scholarship with wide-ranging personal experience. Questions for reflection or discussion make this book a valuable aid to personal or group Bible Study.

Dr John Coutts M.A., B.D., Ph.D.
Formerly Senior Lecturer in Theology,
University of Greenwich

Jim Bryden's study on Paul's letter to the Christians at Ephesus is accessible, but it is nevertheless 'strong meat' in the sense that it draws the reader into deep places of Christian theology and experience.

As one might expect of a man who has spent a lifetime in The Salvation Army, the author explores the great Pauline doctrines of salvation and holiness. The message is always greater than the messenger, but the author/messenger nevertheless shines fresh light on Ephesians through personal witness and reflection.

The language and format of *Journey of Faith: Ephesians* suggest that this book can be used equally effectively in personal study and devotions or for group study and reflection. I would recommend this book for both.

Lieut-Colonel Ian Barr, B.D., M.A
Salvation Army Officer in Retirement

About the Author

As a young teenager and non-churchgoer, Jim had a Damascus Road encounter with Christ which was to lead him into ministry in The Salvation Army. He and his wife Helen were ordained and commissioned as officers in 1968 and served in Scotland, South America, Zimbabwe and England.

Always a pastor and preacher first, he's held a variety of posts as a tutor and lecturer in Bible studies and Theology at The Salvation Army's International College in London and as Training Principal in Zimbabwe.

Besides academic and pastoral responsibilities, for the last six years of active ministry he held the post of Territorial Ecumenical officer for the United Kingdom and Republic of Ireland.

He holds a Bachelor of Divinity degree (Glasgow) and a Masters in Systematic Theology from King's College London.

To Helen,
my darling wife,
and
our two children:

Sheron Kourosh
'Journeying with us'

David Bryden
1964-2009
'With the Lord'

Ephesians

Contents

Ephesians

Introduction

PREPARE TO CLIMB THE HEIGHTS AND WALK IN heavenly places! Enter the message of Ephesians in the power of the Spirit and discover where heaven and earth meet. The mystery of God's eternal will and long-range plan is out in the open. Everything in deepest heaven and planet earth is to be brought together under Christ. The letter to the Ephesians, written by the Apostle Paul, is in a class all of its own and is adorned by such accolades as 'the queen of the epistles' and 'the crown and climax of Pauline theology'. At its heart is God's grace, lavished upon us through Christ! The letter celebrates in prayer and praise that we, without hope and far from God, are made alive in Christ and one with each other. Through him, our minds and hearts are enlightened and empowered by his resurrection so that we radiate his darkness-shattering light. The transformed life of the believer is seen in personal integrity at home and in the community; they promote purity and peace, and fight fearlessly against social and spiritual injustice.

Ephesians

1

Credentials and Challenge

Ephesians 1:1,2

I, Paul, am under God's plan as an apostle, a special agent of Christ Jesus ... to you faithful Christians at Ephesus. I greet you with grace and peace.

Ephesians 1:1,2 (MSG)

WHEN YOU SEND A LETTER, EMAIL OR TEXT TO a friend, you want them to know it's come from you. Writing to a stranger, you would need to say a little more about yourself. Here Paul introduces himself, addresses the readers, then adds a special greeting. There is no personal profile; no hint of exceptional intellect; no reference to special status as a leading figure in the Church of his day. Rather, Paul identifies with all who possess God's gift of grace and peace.

He does, however, declare God-given credentials. As an apostle he's been selected and sent at God's command in the service of Christ Jesus. If you like, he had no say in the matter. God wanted it and that was that.

The people of God are the 'saints' (RSV), or 'faithful Christians' (JBP) – not that they're perfect but, like Paul, they've been called out by God and set apart for his special purpose. They are in the world physically, but spiritually they are above it 'in Christ Jesus'.[1] As Christians, we live in two places at the same time! While we are touched by our culture where the Africans dance in praise to God, the Americans mix patriotism with faith and the British love pageantry and ceremony, as Christians we are defined by Christ.

Today our lives are invaded by secularism and materialism. Political correctness floods and undermines foundational truth. The Christian's faith wrestles with rival takes on life. It's not clear what we can run with and what we can't. Does it have to be this way? No. God's will for us is to be part of Christ[2] and in Christ[3] and to share his grace and peace with all. Hymn writer Colin Fairclough put it this way:

> *Christ of Glory, Prince of Peace,*
> *Let thy life in mine increase;*
> *Though I live may it be shown*
> *'Tis thy life and not my own.*
> *Dwell within, that men may see*
> *Christ, the living Christ, in me.*[4]

---

[1] Quotes from 1:1
[2] See John 15:1ff
[3] See Colossians 3:1-3
[4] *Christ of Glory, Prince of Peace;* Colin Fairclough (1937-2012). See song 573 online: *newsongbook.salvationarmy.org*

QUESTIONS

How would you describe the moral and spiritual qualities of Paul?

Which of these Christian graces do you most desire and why?

What is it that defines a saint of God?

Does sainthood come naturally as a result of the good we do? If not, who/what makes a saint?

In a world invaded by secularism, materialism and political correctness, where foundational Christian truths come under threat, how as believers should we deal with these matters?

2

A Blessed and Glorious Life

Ephesians 1:3-14

And he made known to us the mystery of his will ... to bring all things in Heaven and on earth together under one head, even Christ.

Ephesians 1:9,10

IN THESE VERSES, WE PREPARE TO CLIMB THE heights and walk in heavenly places! We don't arrive at our destination because we planned the route. God alone has made it happen. On arrival, mystery clears like morning mist to reveal the glory of God's eternal plan for all people. Before planets or people existed, '...God chose us to be his very own ... he decided to make us holy in his eyes, without a single fault – we who stand before him covered with his love'[5]. He does this through his Son, and by his Spirit he brings us into Christ.

Paul is on a roll of praise. He's so bowled-over by the God of glory, he doesn't stop for breath. In the Greek, the passage consists of one sentence. It's a prayer; it's a hymn of praise to God, and little wonder! God has opened his home to us. Our name is on the door. We're his adopted sons and daughters. He's lavished his love on us at great

---

[5]   1:4 (TLB)

cost: his only Son's 'blood poured out on the cross'[6]. Why? To destroy sin, save us and make us one with him. We are now on the receiving end of blessing on blessing on blessing! And all because of God's grace.

What is so amazing about grace is not that God gives us something, rather, it is *God's giving us himself!* It's the sheer scale of our salvation and the call to live for God in the world that takes your breath away. The fact that God has made known the mystery of his will which is to bring all things together in Christ is utterly staggering to the apostle. In Christ we're God's chosen family, forgiven sinners. God has singled us out for the special attention of the Holy Spirit. What we have now is awesome; what we will have in Glory is beyond words. There's no holding back the swelling chorus of praise to our God!

How God has lavished his love on us! Lord, how we love you!

---

[6] 1:7 (MSG)

QUESTIONS

To what degree do you think we can, here and now, walk in heavenly places?

What are factors in the life of the believer that generate a 'roll of praise' to God?

What is so amazing about God's grace?

How should we understand 'the mystery of [God's] will'[7]?

---

[7] 1:9

3

Prayer and Power

Ephesians 1:15-23

I keep asking that ... the glorious Father, may give you the Spirit ... so that you may know him better.

Ephesians 1:17

THE INCREDIBLE WORK OF THE SPIRIT SEEN IN the level of love and practical commitment between the believers sends Paul's prayer rocketing. He can't stop thanking God for them. He burns with a powerful longing that God's Spirit will enable them to know Christ deeply in mind and heart: an intelligent, practical and spiritual grasp rolled into one; for the Spirit to open their eyes to see their God-calling, hope and promise in Christ.

The whole experience is immense and glorious for the believer, and God himself is behind it all. His own almighty power that raised Christ from the dead is the same power at work in all who trust him.

This awesome power of God has been placed in Christ so that he is 'far above all rule and authority, power and dominion ... And God [has] placed all things under his feet'[8].

---

[8] 1:21,22

Whatever we might think about the state of our world – its corrupt regimes, the atrocities against humanity, the spread of drug culture, the abuse of women and children – God is sovereign. 'God has placed everything under the power of Christ.'[9] This means what it says: *everything.* Governments, authorities, powers – none have supremacy; all are answerable to Christ. He alone is in charge of all peoples and places.[10] He is without rival or equal.

We live in a world that is simultaneously fallen and free. God did not create robots but human beings. If there's any programming going on, it's learned behaviour. God took a risk in making us as we are. At the same time, he, through his Son, provides more than we need to live the best life ever by accepting his way and not our own. For church community and culture there is none better!

---

[9] 1:22 (JBP)
[10] See Colossians 1:15-20

QUESTIONS

List and comment on the roles of the Spirit as he relates to Christ, God and the life of the believer.

Unpack what Paul has to say about the God's power as it applies to Christ, culture and the believers' commitment.

Do you agree that the world is simultaneously fallen and free? Why or why not?

How should we understand the meaning and significance of the power of God as it applies to Christ and the Church?

4

Dead or Alive?

Ephesians 2:1-10

...though we were dead in our sins God, who is rich in mercy, because of the great love he had for us, gave us life together with Christ – it is, remember, by grace and not by achievement that you are saved.

Ephesians 2:4-6 (JBP)

HERE WE HAVE A CONCISE SUMMARY OF PAUL'S theology on salvation – clear, simple and profound. In ten verses (just one in the Greek), Paul brilliantly encapsulates the devastating consequences of the sinful life, what God has done about it and the response believers need to make.

The first three verses sketch a bleak picture. Because of sin, humans are the 'living dead', subject to a world that ignores God. They're enslaved to the 'ruler of the ... air'[11], to themselves, the 'present evil age'[12] the 'pattern of this world'[13] and at times Satan. When I was young, The Salvation Army labelled it 'worldliness'. It's still around. Why are Nazism and anti-Semitism on the rise? How do

---

[11] 2:2 (NRSV)
[12] Galatians 1:4
[13] Romans 12:2

sexual relations become so distorted? Why is there just beneath the skin of so many a bottled-up rage about to explode? Answer: people are bound to themselves, they are 'following the desires and inclinations of [their] sinful nature'[14] and are alienated from God.

The only way to turn things around is for God to enter the picture and do for humanity what it cannot do for itself: save from sin! We can now rise from death to life, receive a share in Christ's identity and live as God planned. That such extravagant riches from God should be ours, entirely undeserved, is utterly beyond belief. It's his grace and love that brings it all about. Even our ability to *accept* God's gift and exercise faith is itself a gift from him. Our capacity to live and speak and work for him are fuelled and energised by his Spirit's power. This means that me-ism (our pride) is out in the cold.

With all this treasure on board there comes with it the responsibility to share it around. Once I was with some specialists in evangelism. Each concluded we must make greater use of the web and capitalise on modern technology. True, but do people see enough of Christ in us to want a share in God's grace?

---

[14] 1:3 (NLT)

QUESTIONS

Explain what is meant by the text, 'For it is by grace you have been saved, through faith – and this not from yourselves, it is the gift of God – not by works so that no one can boast.'[15]

Name the riches we have if we are in a right relationship with Christ.

The believer is already 'seated ... in the heavenly realms in Christ. ... [He] set us down in highest heaven in company with Jesus.'[16] How does this affect our relationship with God?

---

[15] 2:8
[16] 2:6,7

5

The Living Dead of the Past

Ephesians 2:1-10

But God was merciful! We were dead because of our sins, but God loved us so much he made us alive with Christ, and God's gift of undeserved grace is what saves you.

Ephesians 2:5 (CEV)

THOSE WHO CAN TESTIFY TO BEING 'ALIVE IN Christ' know that they have not naturally arrived at the destiny God has designed for them. None can claim they have been naturally born into the life of God when their mother gave birth. We all, without exception, were still-born. Like it or not, Paul says it as it is to believers:

...that you were mired in that old stagnant life of sin. You let the world, which doesn't know the first thing about living, tell you how to live. You filled your lungs with polluted unbelief, and then exhaled disobedience.

Ephesians 2:1,2 (MSG)

The apostle confesses his failure also:

We all did it, all of us doing what we felt like doing, when we felt like doing it, all of us in the same boat. It's a wonder God didn't lose his

23

> *temper and do away with the whole lot of us.*
> *Instead, immense in mercy and with an*
> *incredible love, he embraced us. He took our*
> *sin-dead lives and made us alive in Christ. He*
> *did all this on his own, with no help from us!*
> *Then he picked us up and set us down in highest*
> *heaven in company with Jesus, our Messiah.*
>
> *Ephesians 2:1-6 (MSG)*

Plainly the apostle regarded the non-Christian life as a spiritual death. Life without God is empty and lost and can become not worth living.

East Enders and other programmes on TV at times illustrate this, where the scriptwriters dish up a diet of conflict, intrigue, broken relationships and thoroughly miserable lives to a hungry populace. Allowing for dramatics which we all love, this is a slice of life that many have come to accept as the norm. It's a style of life by many who have not known God's transforming power. The reality is, God is alien to many. As long as this is the case, they are not in complete control of their own lives. If God is not in your life then someone else is. That someone is – and this is the truth we don't want to hear – Satan. In short, without God's life-changing grace his people are the living dead.

Let us be clear; we're not talking of physical death here but the loss of a spiritual and godly life – the unique life only God can give. The sinful life of humanity is lifeless and motionless in terms of Godward activity. It is a life exposed to the trauma and temptations of the Evil One. As the arch enemy of God, he is opposed to God's authority and seeks to establish his own. Every life not given over to

God is polluted with unbelief and disobedience towards God.

Referring to the two words Paul used for sin here, Dr. John Stott says both words 'express a whole social value-system which is alien to God'. Three broad examples of the destructive power of sin are: Firstly, it permeates, indeed dominates, non-Christian society and holds people in captivity. Secondly, human beings can find themselves dehumanised by political oppression, bureaucratic tyranny and by an outlook on life that is predominately 'secular' i.e. repudiating God beliefs and amoral to the point where they are deaf and blind to absolutes in life. And thirdly, where materialism dominates and the acquisition of accumulating the latest in gadgetry and fashion becomes all-consuming, those in material and spiritual poverty and hunger can easily be bypassed in the race for fame and fortune. Of course, racial discrimination is a very close cousin of this lifestyle, when, taken to extremes, throws up the ugly head of subhuman values.

I have to stress once more a core truth that carries a lifeline not simply of rescue from destruction but the basis upon which the best life of all can be lived. It is that of being 'alive in Christ'! Unless we say yes to God and receive his priceless grace and gift of life in Christ, we remain as good as dead; sin sends us spiralling downward in separation from God, who alone is able to save and make us like Jesus.

In so many ways ours is a wonderful world of beauty and potential. But because it is a *fallen* world, it is flawed and failing. Inevitably that spells trouble. Why? Because it is the opposite of what God's grace can make his people.

QUESTIONS

God's unique designer-life for humanity cannot be achieved by natural effort but only through his life-giving Son Jesus Christ. Do you agree with this statement? If so, why?

_____

_____

_____

Present some examples of the destructive power of sin on people and society, Satan's part, and God's action plan.

_____

_____

_____

_____

Why do you think most people pay no heed to the reality of sin?

_____

_____

_____

_____

6

Sin and Love

Ephesians 2:1-10

You were dead through the trespasses and sins in which you once lived, following the course of this world, following the ruler of the power of the air, the spirit that is now at work among those who are disobedient.

Ephesians 2:1,2 (NRSV)

WHEN REFERRING TO SIN, PAUL USES THE GREEK word *sarx*, which literally means 'flesh'. Let's look together at some aspects of this.

Firstly, our natural state is sinful. This condition leaves God out of the picture. The result is a life taken up with the *me* factor and consequently we say *no* to God. Secondly, our value systems are up the creek. Legitimate human needs might be recognised but the vision is blurred by uncontrollable self-centredness – a factor that is illustrated well in the movies, news programmes and people we rub shoulders with in the 'everyday' of life. This should not be interpreted as judgemental, i.e. a Christian saying, 'I'm better than you.' Rather, where God makes people different from what they are 'naturally' the change is evidenced in their empowerment by God to be and do as the Bible instructs regarding the way of love. Read it for yourself here:

> *If I speak with human eloquence and angelic ecstasy but don't love, I'm nothing but the creaking of a rusty gate.*
>
> *If I speak God's Word with power, revealing all his mysteries and making everything plain as day, and if I have faith that says to a mountain, 'Jump,' and it jumps, but I don't love, I'm nothing.*
>
> *If I give everything I own to the poor and even go to the stake to be burned as a martyr, but I don't love, I've gotten nowhere. So, no matter what I say, what I believe, and what I do, I'm bankrupt without love.*
>
> *Love never gives up.*
> *Love cares more for others than for self.*
> *Love doesn't want what it doesn't have.*
> *Love doesn't strut,*
> *Doesn't have a swelled head,*
> *Doesn't force itself on others, Isn't always 'me first,'*
> *Doesn't fly off the handle,*
> *Doesn't keep score of the sins of others,*
> *Doesn't revel when others grovel,*
> *Takes pleasure in the flowering of truth,*
> *Puts up with anything,*
> *Trusts God always,*
> *Always looks for the best,*

Never looks back,
But keeps going to the end.

Love never dies. Inspired speech will be over
someday; praying in tongues will end;
understanding will reach its limit. We know
only a portion of the truth, and what we say
about God is always incomplete. But when the
Complete arrives, our incompleteness will be
cancelled.

1 Corinthians 13:1-10 (MSG)

How opposite from self-centredness! Where God does not feature in the picture, the search for happiness is on a hiding to nowhere. Try as you may, peace, love and fulfilment are impossible.

The truth is, a life without Christ, the Giver of Life, is flawed and dominated by selfish desire. One of the tragedies of the nineteenth century was the career of Oscar Wilde. A man with a brilliant mind, winning the highest academic honours for his scintillating writing, this charmer with an instinct to be kind was at the mercy of his own insatiable desires. These same desires led him into forms of vice and disgrace which caused him to end up in prison. Behind bars he wrote *De Profundis* in which he stated:

The gods had given me almost everything. But I
let myself be lured into long spells of senseless
and sensual ease. ... Tired of being on the
heights I deliberately went to the depths in
search for new sensation. ... I grew careless of
the lives of others. I took pleasure where it

> *pleased me and passed on. ... I was no longer*
> *the captain of my soul, and did not know it. I*
> *allowed pleasure to dominate me. I ended in*
> *horrible disgrace.*

It's palpably obvious that unbridled, uncontrolled desire is a master of disaster. Usually it glides around and begins to take snapshots of the dangerous and forbidden. Despite what atheists and some humanists say, if human origin is just some freak of nature originating from...

> *...atoms and molecules organised in a*
> *particular way through chance processes of*
> *evolution, then love beauty, good and evil, free*
> *will, reason itself – indeed all that makes us*
> *human and raises us above the rest of the*
> *created order – lose their objectivity.*[17]
>
> *Rodney Holder*

God has placed humanity as his masterpiece in creation. Never will they rise beyond themselves to the fullness of life God has planned they should receive, if they refuse to follow God's way.

---

[17] John Blanchard; *Is God Past His Sell-By Date?;* Evangelical Press (2007); p.124. Blanchard is quoting from Rev. Dr Rodney Holder.

QUESTIONS

'Do your own thing.' 'Be a star way above everyone else.' 'Pay no attention to God.' What does this tell us about the nature of sin?

_____

_____

_____

_____

_____

_____

The best of human effort and sacrifice is no match for God's LOVE as described in 1 Corinthians 13:1-10. What does this truth say to you?

_____

_____

_____

_____

_____

_____

_____

7

Made Alive in Christ

Ephesians 2:1-10

Instead, immense in mercy and with an incredible love, he [Christ] embraced us. He took our sin-dead lives and made us alive in Christ. He did all this on his own, with no help from us!

Ephesians 2:4-6 (MSG)

IN CHRIST THE NIGHT CHANGES TO DAY. THAT old, stagnant, polluted life of our own making changes dramatically. And God had done this with 'no help from us'.

This is something many people don't want to hear. In the world of science, technology, arts, business and so much more, humans like to achieve and make progress on multiple fronts. Of course, and why not? Those who bring God into the equation also recognise that, for all the achievements, there are somethings they cannot do. Humans don't have the know-how to survive beyond death. Humanity on its own can never reach the zenith of what God created them to be. They always fall short. Only by God's help can men and women be what he made them to be: new persons in Christ Jesus.

When someone becomes a Christian, he becomes a brand-new person inside. He is not the same anymore. A new life has begun!

2 Corinthians 5:17 (TLB)

The love of God is the number one theme in Paul's gospel message. Such incredible love is the source and heart of the world's salvation plan that had before time been ever in the heart of God. The cost in terms of suffering and death in God are incalculable.

When Jesus dies, God, far from being impassive, in some creative sense shares in the death of his Son. Jurgen Moltmann's way of exploring this mystery is not to talk about the 'death of God' but 'death *in* [my italics] God'. Moltmann insists that a God who knows nothing of suffering cannot be perfect. Famously he adds:

A God who cannot suffer cannot love either. He is also a loveless being.

The point made here could not be clearer, namely, love is the key to God's suffering which opens the door of hope on all human suffering.

When we are alive in Christ, how rich we are! We who were in a far country, cut off, alien and dead are raised to life in him.

Before it could happen, God willed it should. Before God could save us, he had to assign his one and only Son to that far country of crucifixion and death. Who else could meet God's perfect demands of holiness and justice? Who else could appease the righteous wrath of God, but God himself? Who else could save the lost? Who else could raise the dead?

Only God's Son could make humanity at one with God the Father. Only the Son could save and recreate in his own image. Only the Father could will, the Son obey, the Spirit endorse.

Because the Son laid down his life in obedience to the will of the Father, he is raised to glorious life. Jesus has taken our sin-dead lives and made us alive in himself!

> *Therefore, if anyone is in Christ, the new creation has come: the old has gone, the new is here!*
>
> *2 Corinthians 5:17*

QUESTIONS

What has God done to save his people from sin and death?

_____

_____

_____

_____

_____

For a person to become a Christian what must they do?

_____

_____

_____

When a person is a Christian what changes define them?

_____

_____

_____

_____

_____

8

God's New Society

Ephesians 2:11-22

...now in Christ Jesus you who were ... far away have been brought near.

Ephesians 2:13

WE CAN SOMETIMES FEEL THAT THE 'BEST' AL-ways goes to another; that somehow, we don't count for much. Someone else gets all the breaks and we've got to make do. This is how it was for many in Paul's day. Religion, culture and race were barriers between people. Is it any different today?

Consider religion. When I used to take *The War Cry*[18] into the public houses, often I was accosted with, 'Religion has caused more wars than anything else in the world.' Then, as now, I agree. All major faiths – Jews, Christians, Muslims, Buddhists, Hindus – have spilt innocent blood. Why? They saw the other as the 'outsider', a threat, a rival – even an enemy. The past troubles in Northern Ireland between Protestants and Catholics and the slaughter in Iraq involving Sunni and Shia are frightening examples. Still today we have the war in Syria, which has been going on for seven years and has claimed the lives of more than

---

[18] A weekly publication of The Salvation Army

a quarter of a million people. It is being fought between soldiers who support the president of Syria, Bashar al-Assad, and a group of fighters known as rebels, who don't want him to be in power anymore.[19]

Paul's 'one in Christ'[20] message now deals with a contentious issue in the Church of his day: Jews and Gentiles. At the heart of the dispute was the question of who belongs to God. The Jews regarded themselves as the 'chosen' people to the exclusion of everyone else. It came as a great shock to discover that Gentiles were also included in God's cosmic plan of reconciliation and special relationship with himself. Those who had been 'outsiders', foreigners without covenant promise or hope, were now, through the blood and death of Christ, included in the circle of God's love. Jesus had taken the hostility and hatred upon himself. When he died, it died.

Because of Christ, the walls that divided are smashed to pieces. A building where Christ is the foundation stone stands in its place. As John Stott puts it, we have 'the portrait of an alienated humanity', then 'the portrait of a peace-making Christ' and lastly 'the portrait of God's new society'.

In God's new society Christ is everything and everyone counts for something. No one is out in the cold who is in Christ. No longer is there one favoured people. All are welcome! Together they are invited to form one body of Christ where God's Spirit lives.

---

[19] Source: *BBC Newsround,* 7 April 17

[20] cp. Galatians 3:28

QUESTIONS

What were the barriers in Paul's day to people coming together?

In today's world which prominent factors divide society?

Where does the Christian life figure in forming God's new society?

List and comment on what Christ has done to eliminate alienation and antagonism amongst God's people, give peace and make them 'one in Christ'.

9

God's Open Secret

Ephesians 3:1-13

The Message is accessible and welcoming to everyone, across the board.

Ephesians 3:6 (MSG)

IN TWO SENSES PAUL IS A PRISONER: IN A ROMAN jail awaiting trial before Nero because of his Christ-centred ministry to the Gentiles[21] and as one who deeply adores Christ and finds his real life in Christ. True freedom is total abandonment to Christ. Paul isn't complaining but celebrating. He genuinely counts it an honour to suffer for Christ.[22]

Paul the prisoner remained Paul the preacher. His loss of physical freedom fuelled his passion to proclaim the freedom found only in Christ. We often pray for release from suffering – who can blame us? Yet, if Paul's life is anything to go by, God does his greatest work through our pain and we are drawn more and more into Christ. William Barclay cites F. R. Maltby who said Jesus promised three things to his disciples: '...they would be

---

[21] See Acts 28:16,30
[22] See Philippians 1:3-30

absurdly happy, completely fearless, and in constant trouble'[23]. Paul says:

> God in his grace has given me this work to do for your good. God revealed his secret plan and made it known to me.
>
> *Ephesians 3:2,3 (GNB)*

The best discoveries in life are a gift from God. Topping all of them is the reality that God loves everyone equally in Christ. This is God's open secret. Paul never got over the fact that God chose him, 'less than the least'[24], to be a channel of his grace.[25]

Great conductor Toscanini, briefing an orchestra on a Beethoven symphony, said, 'Gentlemen, I am nothing; you are nothing; Beethoven is everything.' Sadly, today some evangelists are more self-promoting than Christ-adoring. Christ shone through Paul the way he did because Paul regarded himself as nothing, while Christ was everything. We too have been entrusted with 'the unsearchable riches of Christ'[26] to be shared in service to others.

In the 1960s the *Joystrings* (a beat group formed within The Salvation Army) famously sang their songs in churches, in theatres, on TV and in the red light district of Soho, London. An unforgettable song was *It's an Open*

---

[23] William Barclay; *The Daily Study Bible;* St Andrew Press (2002)

[24] 3:8

[25] See Galatians 2:7,9; Romans 15:15

[26] 3:8 (ESV)

Secret, which said we can 'know God's loving-kindness'.[27] God's message 'is accessible and welcoming to everyone, across the board'[28]. Our world is dying to hear God's open secret. Only those who place Christ first can tell it as it is, whatever the cost.

---

[27] You can google 'Joy Strings' to see and hear them for yourself.

[28] 3:6 (MSG)

QUESTIONS

Paul declared himself to be a slave to Christ and counted it an honour to suffer for him. What truths can we draw from this as followers of Christ?

_____

_____

_____

The apostle Paul received from the Spirit a direct revelation concerning the mystery hidden for centuries. What was this mystery/secret that is now out in the open?

_____

_____

_____

Today some Christians are more 'self-promoting than Christ adoring'. With Paul, it was radically different. Explain the difference and what characteristics should define the people of God.

_____

_____

_____

_____

10

God's Treasure Beyond Measure

Ephesians 3:14-21

I pray that out of his glorious riches he may strengthen you with power through his Spirit in your inner being.

Ephesians 3:16

MY WIFE AND I VISITED PHOENIX, ARIZONA IN the USA. One day we watched as an eagle soared and glided with great ease high up in the prairie sky. In this prayer, Paul is flying, as it were, in heavenly places. Like an eagle carried on the thermo, he is able to view the vast, extravagant dimensions of the riches of Christ! Chest bursting with joy, he strives to articulate the indescribable.

Paul can hardly believe it! Those far from God, dubbed the 'outsiders' are now made alive in Christ. Each has priceless access into the very presence of Almighty God. There is only one way to respond to such truth: fall on your knees before the Father of all. As a Jew he was required to stand and pray, but how could he? The reality is mind-boggling. Instead, he prostrates himself before God's glorious majesty! When we pray, the posture is less important than the passion, pleading and worship we bring to it.

Paul longs for the Ephesians to be 'rooted and established in love'[29]. It is a prayer that through the Spirit's power, they may know the boundless depths and dimensions of Christ's love.[30] Only the Spirit can make it happen. Only the Spirit empowers and enables the believer to know the 'deep things of God'[31]. Only the Spirit brings us into line with God's will. God's love is the source by which believers are nourished. To know Christ's love is to be transformed by that love and share in the very fullness of God!

As children of our loving heavenly Father, we are urged to, 'Reach out and experience the breadth! Test its length! Plumb the depths! Rise to the heights! Live full lives, full in the fullness of God.'[32]When this happens, the drive to reach others is powerful: to bless those who hate us, bring hope to the hopeless, food to the hungry and life to the dying. On us the Spirit has lavished God's treasure beyond measure!

---

[29] 3:17
[30] See verses 16 and 19
[31] 1 Corinthians 2:10-12
[32] 3:18,19 (MSG)

QUESTIONS

Describe the 'big picture' of God you see in this passage.

_____

_____

_____

_____

God's 'treasure beyond measure' is given through the Spirit's power so that we may know/share in the deepest level of Christ's love. What does this mean to you?

_____

_____

_____

The world is broken, divided, lost. The church is made up of many shapes and sizes. All varieties have a part to play in the body of Christ. What needs to happen to unite the people of God in Christ and be effective in faith and mission?

_____

_____

_____

_____

11

Forward as One

Ephesians 4:1-16

I want you to get out there and walk – better yet, run! – on the road God called you to travel.

Ephesians 4:1 (MSG)

HAVING DEALT WITH THE HEART OF THE Christian faith, Paul now looks for evidence of its practical application in daily life. 'No passage is more descriptive of the church in action,' says the NIV Commentary. The picture is of the body of Christ, made of many parts. The appeal is for movement and maturity. It's time for infants in the faith to grow up. How well I remember my granddaughter of five singing with gusto, 'Move it! Move it! Move it!' There are no diversions, no shortcuts, just one way forward: Christ's way.

We are all called to mirror Christ's humility, discipline and, above all, love. It's not a case of putting up with each other but of looking out for others. We should take second place.[33] We're to be radiant with gentle sensitivity, to practise patience and, in the words of J. Chrysostom, 'have a wide and big soul'. The heart of it all is this: being with Christ means loving like Christ. Most of us struggle with

---

[33] See Philippians 2:5-8

this requirement. Why? The concept in the song *I Did it My Way* is why. But if, like Paul, we forget about ourselves and become Christ's prisoner, we will move forward and take others with us.

In moving forward, we do so as one:

> *One Master, one faith, one baptism, one God and Father of all, who rules over all, works through all, and is present in all. Everything you are and think and do is permeated with Oneness.*

Ephesians 4:5,6 (MSG)

The division in the Church is largely caused by those who think they have a monopoly on truth. Individualism in faith is flawed and dangerous. We all need each other. As F. F. Bruce says, 'The higher reaches of the Christian life cannot be attained in isolation from one's fellow believers.'

The grace of Christ gifts God's people with power by the Spirit. They have different roles: prophets, evangelists, pastors and teachers in parallel ministry. All matter. All have a part to play for all belong to the one body of Christ. By the reality of God's truth and love, we go forward as one.

QUESTIONS

What Christian graces must the believer nurture and aspire to if he/she is to go grow in faith and go forward together with others as one in the body of Christ?

_____

_____

The body of Christ is made up of many parts. Each member is assigned a different task. What are these roles and where does the Spirit figure in making things happen to bring about unity in the faith and maturity in Christ?

_____

_____

All too often the people of God find themselves snared by discord and rivalry, where humility is crushed by unholy ambition, and a pompous 'I'm better than you' and 'I know best' attitude dominates. What lessons can we draw from this passage on how to dispel division and move forward as one in Christ?

_____

_____

_____

12

Throw Away the Old, Put on the New

Ephesians 4:17-24

Fling off the dirty clothes of the old way of living, which were rotted through and through ... put on the clean fresh clothes of the new life which was made by God's design.

Ephesians 4:22-24 (JBP)

I LOVE IT WHEN I PUT ON A CLEAN, FRESHLY ironed shirt – the fragrance, the feel. By contrast, one cold winter's day my wife helped peel off the foul-smelling rags of a street gentleman, while her friend bathed his swollen wounded feet. A hot meal, new clothes, and his eyes shone with hope.

Paul is dealing here with two kinds of life. One is futile, without meaning, promise or even reality. Pride and self-centredness have pushed God out of the picture. The result is that the light has been turned off.

They can't think straight anymore. Feeling no pain, they let themselves go in sexual obsession, addicted to every sort of perversion.

Ephesians 4:19 (MSG)

The other life is one transformed in union with Christ. Those living it walk in the light of God, their minds renewed. They have stripped off 'the old way of living ... [and] put on the clean fresh clothes of the new life'[34] from God.

We live in a society that promotes fame and fortune, and values popularity and pleasure more than sacrifice and service. The media industry both informs and shapes us with news, films and TV shows, and singers, actors and talk-show hosts along with sport celebrities occupy centre stage.

Sadly, sexual promiscuity and violence to women and children are all too common. Untamed desire craves more and more satisfaction, and self-centredness rules too many people. Although sexuality and pleasure are not bad in themselves, they are gifts from God to be used in ways that honour him – wrongly used, they can become masters exerting a tyrannical power.

What's the answer? It is to sign up for learning at the feet of Christ and become a new person by his power. God calls us to throw away the old and put on the new, to exchange rags for royal robes. This way the old 'me' gives way to a new me.[35] And what is the new me? The very character of God in me!

---

[34] 4:22,24 (JBP)
[35] See 4:22-24; also, Colossians 3:9-11; Romans 6:3,6

QUESTIONS

Paint a word picture of the life, mindset and practices of people whose pride and self-centredness have barred them from the life of God.

Ideally, the believer is one who has thrown away the old life and put on the new. In reality, a tug-of-war exists between the two. What steps must we take if there's to be less of the 'old me' and more of the 'new me' in Christ?

Have you experienced God reproducing his character in you? In what way?

13

New Life of Love

Ephesians 4:25-5:2

...live a life of love, just as Christ loved us and gave himself up for us.

Ephesians 5:2 (MSG)

TELL THE TRUTH. KEEP YOUR HEAD. GIVE UP stealing and get a job. Mind your language. It sounds like a list of instructions. It is. We're talking ethics here. The Christian life based on Christ's love is always accountable for its behaviour. Its top priority, according to the NIV Commentary, is to 'reject what destroys community and promote what builds community'. This community 'is intimately related to each other in Christ', although at times you'd hardly think so, the way some people go on. Despite God's truth and love, Paul declares their track record a failure. Let's be honest, at times we're all poor examples at home and unattractive adverts for Christianity in society.

Instead of reflecting the new being in Christ, we sometimes lack transparency, telling people what they want to hear if it works to our advantage, and shrinking from the truth when it's costly. Sometimes we exaggerate to enhance ourselves at someone else's expense, distorting reality. And, as John Mackay says, lying to ourselves or to others 'delivers a stab into the very vitals of the body of Christ ... there is no place in the Christian ethic for the well-intentioned lie'[36]. Only truth builds people and society. It comes from God. Without it, nothing's sure, nothing survives.

Jesus says it as it is:

> *You are truly my disciples if you remain faithful*
> *to my teachings. And you will know the truth,*
> *and the truth will set you free.*
>
> *John 8:31,32 (NLT)*

Addressing Christians, Paul says there's to be no more bitterness, rage, anger, brawling, slander or malice. Anger here is not referring to anger in response to such things as poverty, injustice, lies, racism and abuse. Rather it's the destructive sort that lashes out with harsh, uncontrolled temper. When two people fail to reconcile their differences, it grieves God the Holy Spirit, invites hostility and destroys human relations. Such antagonism is a vice and an enemy to God's people.

How do we deal with an enemy, either from within or without? With kindness, understanding, forgiveness and, above all, love – the 'same kind of love which Christ gives us and which he perfectly expressed when he gave himself up for us in sacrifice to God'[37]. In this life of love, we are to 'watch what God does, and then you do it'[38].

---

[36] Quoted from Klyne Snodgrass; *The NIV Application Commentary: Ephesians;* Zondervan (1996).

[37] 4:32; 5:1,2 (JBP)

[38] 5:1 (MSG)

QUESTIONS

Why is what you think, say and do in your Christian life
of vital importance to others and God?

In the lives of those who follow Christ, where is anger
permissible and where is it not?

What is involved in living a life of love to others and God?

Paint a word picture of behaviours that are destructive to
human relations and those which are constructive.

14

You are the Light in the Lord

Ephesians 5:3-14

The bright light of Christ makes your way plain. So no more stumbling around. Get on with it!

Ephesians 5:9 (MSG)

THE STARTING LINE IS THE LIGHT AND LOVE OF Christ. It will take believers to the finishing point. The in-between bit can be messy. Christians, says Paul, are surrounded with alien lifestyles: sexual promiscuity, sickening greed, dirty talk. These must not form any part of their lives. Once 'darkness', now 'light', they are to do what pleases Christ.

This passage could have been written to members of any church. Why, even in Christian fellowships, is there sometimes sexual sin, bad language and greed? Sexual sin trades on pride, power and pleasure. Foul talk lowers the moral temperature. Before you know it, obscenities and course joking are acceptable. Untamed desire leads to greed for possessions and power. Such greed cramps and masters our every move. The advertising and gambling industries profit from the 'must have, must own' of our lives. Twisted sex, dirty words and selfish living are all variations of idolatry. God will judge severely, warns Paul.

Into all of this comes Christ's transforming light, shining through his people.[39] From him we receive a new being. We are stamped with his identity. Love, goodness and truth define us as 'we shine like stars in the universe'[40], confronting the darkness of our street and society.

We must steer clear of the dark side, and reach out to people, practising distinctiveness, not separation. As the saying has it, we must 'hate the sin, but love the sinner'. Only God, by his light and truth, is able to destroy the power of sin and save the world and its people.[41]

We have here a wake-up call. The race is on, there's no time to lose. The light is shining. The darkness can't escape it. God's children of light see things as they really are. We live with the danger of the world's values rubbing off on us but we know how to overcome: by putting Christ first! That way we are light in the Lord.

---

[39] Ephesians 5:8
[40] Philippians 2:15 (NIV, 1994 edition)
[41] See Romans 6:19-23; John 3:16,19-21.

QUESTIONS

List and comment on the aspects of the dark side of humanity that opposes God's message of the light and love of Christ.

Based upon Paul's message here, what action should be taken by the fellowship when dealing with any member(s) who disregard Christian morals?

What does it mean that the believer is 'light in the Lord'?

15

Mind How You Go

Ephesians 5:15-21

*Make the best of your time ... firmly grasp what
you know to be the will of God.*

Ephesians 5:16,17 (JBP)

WE LIVE IN DESPERATE TIMES. WHAT'S NEW?
Does human nature ever change? Not unless God does the
job. The apostle Paul is pressing here for believers to make
the best use of time. The clock is ticking. The days are evil.
Lives are wasted on drunkenness 'which leads to
debauchery'[42]. This is mindless and irresponsible waste.[43]
Worse still, such a life bypasses being 'filled with the
Spirit'[44] of God.

Alternatively, where the Spirit flows through us,
everything else falls into place. Inspiration to, 'Sing and
make music'[45] pleasing to God springs from our amazing
walk with him. Christ is the centre and circumference of
everything. Knowing and doing God's will, not our own,
is the greatest thing in the world. The outcome is

---

[42] 5:18
[43] See Romans 13:12,13
[44] 5:18
[45] 5:19

exuberant praise and 'thanks to God' twinned with mutual respect and submission to each other.[46]

Our society is in a big hurry. Gadgetry does much for us but we're busier than ever. Our lives are packed with activity but how much time do we give to God? Some indulge themselves in alcohol. While consumption of alcoholic beverage is not a sin, drunkenness is. Whether binge drinking or drunken drivers, the end result can be devastating. The point made by Paul is that debauchery results from excessive and wasteful indulgence.

The truth is, we are made for God's Spirit to inhabit. All we are, all we hope to be, is brought into focus by the Spirit, who is no optional extra or secondary being in the Godhead. He's no less than the Bringer of Life! When he comes to us, he is not alone. God the Father and Son are with him, in us. When this happens, we are in the centre of God's will. For this reason, we act with wisdom, make the best use of our time, revere one another and celebrate in a chorus of praise and thanksgiving to our great God.

---

[46] See Colossians 3:15-17; 4:2; 1 Peter 1:3-5; Philippians 2:3; Matthew 23:12

QUESTIONS

Christians are required to live by a strict code of conduct. What sort of things does the apostle insist upon if we are to be wise and godly?

When it comes to living for God, what counts above everything else?

Being filled with the Spirit is readily linked to music and song. Do you think that praise to God in this form of expression in worship is important? If so, why?

16

Love Like Christ

Ephesians 5:22-33

Husbands, love your wives, just as Christ loved the church and gave himself up for her ... and the wife must respect her husband.

Ephesians 5:25,33 (MSG)

WHAT MAKES A SUCCESSFUL MARRIAGE? WHEN a church goes wrong, how can it be put right? Two questions, one answer. For the couple, for the community of faith, the answer lies in loving the way Christ loves. A fragmented church, like a fractured relationship, is due to the absence of Christ. Paul's primary subject here is not really marriage; he uses that as an analogy for 'the marriage of Christ and his Church'[47]. The love of Christ, his saving work and his constant care for the Church is pre-eminent.

Does this mean the weddings we've attended were wrong when this passage was read: 'Wives, submit to your husbands ... Husbands, love your wives'[48]? No. Although these verses might appear to order that husbands should rule and wives submit, this is a gross misinterpretation.

---

[47] 5:32 (JBP)
[48] 5:22,25

Husbands have no privileged position. Wives are not inferior. At work here is mutual submission and support. 'The husband provides leadership to his wife the way Christ does to his church, not by domineering but by cherishing.'[49] Loving her as much as he loves himself and as much as Christ loves the Church is a huge responsibility.

And wives are to understand and support their husbands in ways similar to the way the Church submits to Christ. It has nothing to do with one marriage partner being better than the other. It has everything to do with equal yet distinct roles in Christ. In marriage or being single, all Christians are to act towards each other as Christ acts.[50]

In our relationship with Christ, the Church and each other, there's only one head and that's Christ. But while head, he's also the servant of all, and so must we be to each other.[51] If we are to love like Christ then we should take note:

> *Christ's love makes the church whole. His words evoke her beauty. Everything he does and says is designed to bring the best out of her, dressing her in dazzling white silk, radiant with holiness.*
>
> *Ephesians 5:26-28 (MSG)*

---

[49] 5:24 (MSG)
[50] See Romans 12:10
[51] See Matthew 20:26-28

QUESTIONS

To love like Christ is a tall order. Paul promotes the ideal marriage for its own merit. More importantly, he uses the bond in marriage as an analogy of Christ's love for the church. Provide some examples of Christ's love, how it is evident in everyday life and Christian marriage.

_____

_____

_____

_____

_____

Looking at the depth of Christian marriage as expressed here, what are the gems in this relationship to be treasured and the promises that must be kept?

_____

_____

_____

_____

_____

_____

_____

17

A Family in the Lord

Ephesians 6:1-4

*Children, obey your parents in the Lord ...
'Honour your father and mother ... that it may
go well with you' ... Fathers, do not exasperate
your children ... bring them up in the training
and instruction of the Lord.*

Ephesians 6:1-4 (MSG)

'APART FROM RELIGIOUS INFLUENCE,' WRITES DR
Billy Graham, 'the family is the most important unit in
society ... [it] can never exert its proper influence while
ignoring the biblical standard.'[52] The standard is Christ.
We are not talking merely about ethics but about family
life being 'in Christ', with parents exerting patient and
loving discipline 'in the Lord'. In that way, children can
model their lives on their parents' good and godly
influence.

Where fathers 'exasperate' their children, they're
clearly failing to live up to the high ideal outlined in these
verses.

---

[52] George Sweeting; *Great Quotes and Illustrations;* Word
Publishing (1990)

As for the children, they are not free to have it all their own way. Like it or not, they are commanded to obey their parents – something entirely justified where parents are modelling Christ to their children. Nineteenth century evangelist D. L. Moody said, 'A man ought to live so that everybody knows he is a Christian and most of all, his family ought to know.'[53] Sadly, at times we operate a double persona: one private, one public. The 'nice' person people see in public can be quite different at home, where our loved ones see us as we really are. All of us adults and children must own up to our failures and allow the Lord to guide us.

Some Christian parents can rejoice that their adult children follow the Lord's leading. Others, despite their poured-out love and prayers over the years, suffer the ongoing heartbreak of a child who has turned their back on Christ, sometimes to the extent of rejecting all their parents stand for. Why? Only God knows.

Homes in which family members use and abuse each other for their own ends release into the wider community an explosive cocktail of anger, violence and abuse. 'Sins of the fathers' are sometimes passed on from generation to generation. When parents fail, often the children do so as well. John Locke said, 'Parents wonder why the streams are bitter when they themselves have poisoned the fountain.'

The best family is one 'in the Lord', characterised by mutual respect, integrity of faith and, above all, love.

---

[53] George Sweeting; *Great Quotes and Illustrations;* Word Publishing (1990)

QUESTIONS

What do you consider to be the *musts* for a family in the Lord?

Where families fail and fall apart, what are the most common factors that contribute to that and how should these be tackled?

What steps may be taken on the part of parents whose adult child chooses to turn away from God?

18

I Honour You as I Honour Christ

Ephesians 6:5-9

Serve wholeheartedly, as if you were serving the Lord, not people ... slave or free.

Ephesians 6:7,8 (MSG)

IT IS ESTIMATED THAT IN PAUL'S DAY MORE than a third of the population were slaves. The culture and economy rode on the backs of those with few or no rights. Many were treated harshly, some condemned to death with no appeal. By contrast others held key posts in institutions and households. In both poor and rich families, some slaves were regarded as valued members of the family.

Who owned whom? Legally, the slave was in the service of his or her master. But in Christian households both slave and free were bound to Christ himself. Each was required to submit to the other. In that respect, they were no different from everyone else in the Christian community.[54]

By this, the slavery system was stood on its head. Each was 'to obey the real master, Christ'[55]. Submission on the

---

[54] See 5:21
[55] 6:5 (MSG)

part of a slave owner was revolutionary. Paul insisted that all believers, like himself, should be slaves, not of men, but of Christ – the one who made himself nothing.[56] Had this ideal happened, the Greco-Roman world might have been so different and the shameful transatlantic trade in human cargo might never have taken place.

Dr Martin Luther King's 'I have a dream...' speech on 28 August 1963 urged, 'Let freedom ring [for all].' The fight for freedom goes on. People are still dehumanised. Insidious forces are at work. The white slave trade and illicitly obtained human body parts today plunge thousands of people into misery and despair. Far from honouring human dignity, acknowledging that each person possesses God's image, trafficked people are perceived as objects of sexual pleasure and cheap labour.

The Christian's work ethic and human relations happen in the presence of Christ. Whatever we do to others, we do to Christ.[57] The believer is not favoured above the non-believer. Each has equal standing before God.[58] All should have the best we can give. Unless we respect and value all, we cannot honour Christ. Now there's a challenge and no mistake!

---

[56] See 1 Corinthians 7:21-23; Romans 1:1,2; Philippians 2:7
[57] See Matthew 25:40
[58] See James 2:1-13

QUESTIONS

Living in a day when one-third of the population were in servitude, Paul urges Christians to serve their masters like they were serving Christ. Equally, the owner was to do likewise. What does this say to you about culture and faith?

_____

_____

_____

_____

_____

Modern slavery and the dehumanising of people for sexual pleasure, their body parts and cheap labour are a curse on humanity and a blasphemy against God's image on every human being. How should the Christians deal with this injustice?

_____

_____

_____

_____

_____

19

The Fight Goes On

Ephesians 6:10-13

God is strong, and he wants you strong ... to stand up to everything ... This is for keeps, a life-or-death fight to the finish against the Devil and all his angels.

Ephesians 6:10,11,13 (MSG)

PUT ON GOD'S ARMOUR AND HIS CHARACTER-istics, and you become a new you, 'like God in true righteousness and holiness'[59]. God's designer attire fits us perfectly. His power and strength can be ours, not just to help us 'feel good' but to do battle against what William Shakespeare has called 'the slings and arrows of outrageous fortune'[60]. We must take evil seriously, not playing around with magic, musing on Satan or dabbling in astrology.

We refuse to rest while the world bleeds. The open wounds of oppression and exploitation, the brutalising and bestial treatment of human beings, the shame of the starving and the horror of the lost must grab our attention. We cannot be a Christian without being a soldier.

---

[59] 4:24
[60] *Hamlet,* Act III, Scene 1

Who's the enemy? Not people, not authorities, but schemes, philosophies, systems and ideologies designed to work against humanity, devaluing and destroying it. The fight that goes on is the fight against evil and the evil one. Everything from mass murder of other ethnic groups to personal failure, declaring, 'I wasn't myself when I did that,' reveals the undeniable reality of evil.

In modern culture the reality of the devil is less acceptable than once it was. This is not a good thing. As someone has said, 'Satan's greatest weapon is to convince the world he does not exist.' This much is certain: the power of darkness is a time bomb which can bring destruction to nations and individuals, though in the end it will be defeated.[61]

What of now? This is God's world. Only he is in charge. Forces ranged against him are being, and will be, defeated.[62] Never forget that Satan, unlike God, can't be everywhere at once. His powers are limited. His days are numbered. Look to God. Don't focus on the evil one. When we turn our eyes from God, blindness takes us over. Paul urges us to be 'strong in the Lord and his mighty power'[63]. The sounds of the Christ's victory vibrate in our hearts. Yes, the fight goes on, but the victory has already been won!

---

[61] See Matthew 25:41
[62] See Luke 10:18; Revelation 12:7-17
[63] 6:10

QUESTIONS

The old hymn, 'Onward Christian soldiers marching as to war', very strongly makes the case that followers of Christ are in a war zone. Who is the enemy here? How should we deal with the enemy?

Should we take the reality of Satan seriously? If so, how does this impact on the way we deal with thinking and practices that degrade and destroy the fight for justice and peace?

20

Armour of Protection, Power and Prayer

Ephesians 6:14-20

Stand firm ... take the ... sword of the Spirit, which is the word of God. And pray in the Spirit.

Ephesians 6:14,17,18

ACTION STATIONS! NOT ONLY IS THERE NO discharge in this war, there is no going it alone either. The enemy is fierce and cunning and the challenges on every side call for constant vigilance. No one can win, or even survive, without the correct equipment. No victory will be secured without the Spirit's power. Prayer and the gospel are the most formidable weapons of God's soldier.

Like soldiers, we are to mount a serious campaign, take the high ground and hold it at all costs. This is not for the faint-hearted. Paul uses the analogy of the Roman soldier with his armour and sword. The soldier's belt, breastplate, footwear, shield, helmet and sword signify truth, righteousness, peace, faith, salvation and God's Word. Protection from enemy attack and power to defeat the enemy rest on two factors: God's protective armour[64] and the 'sword of the Spirit, which is the word of God'.

Standing firm, engaging the enemy and winning the battle calls for commitment to prayer. Paul's 'pray in the Spirit'[65] is not about speaking in tongues. Rather, he connects it with being filled with the Spirit's strength and persevering when the going gets tough.[66] Prayer also produces the power to be fearless when proclaiming the mystery of the gospel,[67] which is made known by God through revelation.

May God help us to take our stand for Christ, boldly and in the power of his mighty Spirit! May he teach us not just to pray our 'wish list' but to identify with his own will and purpose in every circumstance of life. Someone has said, 'Prayer is a kind of spiritual breathing.' We need to pray not just in our quiet 'set-aside' times but also through the toil and grind of dark, doubt-filled days, and in the thick of battle when peace is a distant dream. May we 'not be anxious', for the Spirit is with us and his peace guards our hearts.[68]

---

[64] See Isaiah 11:5; 59:17; 52:7

[65] 6:18

[66] See 3:16; 5:18; Philippians 4:6,7

[67] See 6:19,29

[68] See Philippians 4:6,7; Romans 8:26

QUESTIONS

List and comment on the significance of the armour of God.

What makes praying in the Spirit and God's Word indispensable for the soldier of God?

21

The Message and the Messenger

Ephesians 6:21-23

Tychicus ... my good friend ... is certainly a dependable servant of the Master! I've sent him ... to cheer you on in your faith. Good-bye, friends. Love mixed with faith be yours from God the Father and from the Master, Jesus Christ. Pure grace and nothing but grace be with all who love our Master, Jesus Christ.

Ephesians 6:21-24 (MSG)

WHEN YOU SEND A LETTER OR PACKAGE AND want to be sure it arrives intact, you pay an extra cost for 'special delivery'. The apostle Paul knew that Tychicus was someone of exceptional character and Christian standing, and therefore chose him as his messenger to Ephesus. The letter would be delivered by hand, along with a verbal report on the imprisoned Paul in Rome.[69]

Typically, Paul ignores his own pain as a prisoner to cheer and encourage the believers. He knew about suffering but also knew God would always be there. He

---

[69] See 6:21,22

further knew how to forget about himself and focus on the pain of others with Christ-like compassion.[70]

When, as a young man, I was commissioned as a Salvation Army officer in London's Royal Albert Hall, I heard the then leader of The Salvation Army, General Frederick Coutts, utter words which are forever indelibly printed on my mind and which subsequently enriched my ministry: 'The message is greater than the messenger!' That's it. When the messenger delivers the message, taking Christ as his model, then peace, love and grace reach their target.

The end of this letter links with the beginning.[71] The benediction emphasises 'God the Father and the Lord Jesus Christ'[72] as the source of peace, love, faith and grace. The believers have one glorious God and Father and are blessed beyond measure. God has given us all we need. We are all called and commissioned to live out in action to others what we have become in Christ.

May 'pure grace and nothing but grace be with all who love our Master, Jesus Christ'[73].

---

[70] See 4:1; 2 Corinthians 1:4
[71] cp. 1:3
[72] 6:23,24
[73] 6:24 (MSG)

QUESTIONS

What is it about the message of the gospel that makes it unique?

Paul suffered much in his Christian journey. What do you think this did for him, his faith and ministry?

Why is the message greater than the messenger?

Prayer

Lord, thank you for giving us yourself without reserve!

Teach us to follow your example.

Grant us your grace that we may give ourselves away to others and, in service, see Christ in all.

Amen.

Contact the Author

To contact the author, please write to:

Jim Bryden
c/o Onwards and Upwards Publishers Ltd.
3 Radfords Turf
Exeter
EX5 7DX

Or send an email to:

jamesandhelenbryden@icloud.com

More information about the author can be found
on the book's web page:

www.onwardsandupwards.org/journey-of-faith-ephesians

What Shall I Read Next?

Learn more about the life of Jesus – who he was, what he did and his death and resurrection – with sixteen daily readings, explanations and applications, as well as optional short exercises to help you dig deeper into the Word.

ISBN: 978-1-78815-706-3
RRP: £6.99

Learn more about God's plan to reach the world through the church, the Body of Christ. Jim shows how believers are called to live out their lives and share the gospel with perseverance and faithfulness, with the promise of a heavenly reward.

ISBN: 978-1-78815-557-1
RRP: £6.99